Ocean's Anger

BRENDA J. STEMMLER

Book
Collaborators
Your Story, Our Network

OCEAN'S ANGER
Copyright © 2025 Brenda J. Stemmler.

ISBN 978-1-967362-35-6 (Paperback)
ISBN 978-1-967362-37-0 (Ebook)
ISBN 978-1-967362-36-3 (Hardcover)

Printed in the United States of America

Contents

FINAL SAY

I stood in the shadows
waiting for a relationship
that would never happen…
Eager to please him…
Wanting to understand…
Why did anger fill his life?
Death had taken him before
my questions were answered.
Now anger flooded my heart,
as my father's silence was felt
Like the back of his hand so often
was. I cried out with the need to
Understand, but my father had the final say!

As I walked out into the water of the Atlantic Ocean, I suddenly realized how much power was in front of me. With my girlfriend coaxing me onward, I did, but suddenly, as my fears grew, I turned for the shores I had slowly left behind.

Then in one rushing moment, the power of the waves knocked me to the ocean's bottom, sending pain through my body. I struggled violently to reach the surface as thoughts of my childhood quickly flooded into my mind. My heart pounded like a drum each time my body hit the bottom. The water held me down. I kicked at the liquid, trying to fight my way to the surface. Each time my legs would touch the floor, the water overpowered them.

"Don't get up," a voice yelled, but I have to. I have to get to the shores…No, I have to get away from him…

Flashes of my father confused my mind. Where was I? How did my father get here? Somebody please help me, I tried to scream, but the water filled my mouth. My jaw ached with pain. Could I get up now without being hit again? I struggled again to reach the surfaces, but darkness swept me down. Where was the day? How did I get here? Why wouldn't he quit hitting me? The final blows knocked me against the wall. Pain was now greater than ever, but there was silence now. What had happened to me? The voice was deaf to my ears. "Hold on," I kept telling myself. "There is help somewhere, and the pain will soon be over." A voice in the distance soon broke through my silent tomb, and I felt the bottom return under my feet.

"Are you all right?" Lisa said as she grabbed me under my arms, helping me to the shore.

"Yes," I quickly answered, not knowing if I was then suddenly, I felt the pain again, blood dripped from my leg onto the white sand, as fast as the ocean's mouth could swallow it up. The ocean's sharp floor had put its mark on me. A mark that would leave a scar, much like the scars of my childhood. My head throbbed with the thoughts that had flashed through my mind. What had happened to me?

"I think I will sit out for a while," I whispered to Lisa; I hadn't fully caught my breath yet.

"Okay, but tomorrow you can try again."

"Tomorrow," I thought to myself as I remembered the thoughts that had flooded my mind while the water was holding me under. Tomorrow had been my greatest fear as a child. What would tomorrow bring…?

My father would be gone to work by the time I would get out of bed, so I knew my day would have a chance, but when he would arrive home, the day could explode in a matter of minutes. His moods were like the tides of the ocean, high and low, so you didn't want to get in his way, or you would feel the impact of his words and his hands. I had to listen closely to the sounds his voice would spill out, because my world was not deaf to some sounds. My father had left his hand marks on my life when he slapped me upside the head with his fist. The dishes had been left dirty, and I got the blame for someone else's job not being finished. After the pain of that day left my body, I knew I would have to be on guard for more of the same, but now my efforts to survive were harder, because sometimes I couldn't hear his heavy footsteps on my path.

The day ended with my first introduction to the ocean, but the reminder of my childhood was not gone. I thought that I had dealt with the hard blows of it after my father's death. Now the power of the ocean had brought back the memories.

It was not until the death of my father on September 2, 1984, that I realized how much anger had become a big part of my life. Death had taken my father before I could understand all the things that had gone on in my life. As a child growing up, I always stood in the shadow, waiting for a relationship that would never happen. But what I did get was the back of his hand whenever things didn't go his way. Eager to please him and stay away from the punishment, I would always volunteer to do things for him that my mother or other brothers and sisters wouldn't do.

I recall one time when the weather began to change during the day to rain and snow, I took my father's coat and gloves to him at work. It was a good mile walk for a young girl. He never even thanked me. It didn't matter what I did for him; he always seemed to use me as his whipping post.

As the years moved on. I married the year I graduated in 1969. The same year, my father discovered that he would no longer be able to work. His anger became stronger and stronger, and I could soon see the toll it had on my family. Out of his need to find a way to cope with his problems, he came to my home in tears one day. He wanted to know why he had been put through so much suffering. This was the man, as a child, I would do anything for just to have his fatherly love, and now, he was asking me for help. He frightened me, because I wanted to be there for him, but I had to ask myself, "What would the outcome be if I gave him the wrong answers." This was also the man who had no answers for my problems when I needed him. I felt angered by his presence. Years and years went by with more and more anger building up inside of me. I could not understand why it had been so hard for my father to love me. Love was a word I didn't understand, but I knew somehow it wasn't the violence my dad so often showed. When my father's death came, it was as if he had taken that final blow. He had died without ever once telling me he loved me. All the years of trying to understand him were now laid to rest and covered over with dirt. How would I get the answers to my unanswered questions? My dad, like always had had the final…

"Candy, let's go for a walk on the beach," Lisa suggested.

"The moon is full and the air is fresh."

Haunted by the memories that had invaded my mind earlier that day, I thought that this could give me a different look at things. I was right; the ocean at night could make me forget about everything and anything. The white cascades washed over the shores, forming new patterns in the sand. Trails of sea shells were left behind, but not for long. Treasure hunters sought to find whatever had been left from each time that so softly touched at the ocean shore.

"Isn't the ocean beautiful at night?" Lisa asked. "How could anyone not find the beauty in it?" she continued.

"Beauty was not my first impression," I answered. But you are right. It does have a certain beauty about it."

We walked about two miles down the shore. The tranquil flow of the ocean's movement brought a certain comfort to my mind. Our walk was the time I needed to put the day in perspective.

Pieces

A mirror reflecting
what is housed inside.
No cares, No love.
Shattered by the pain,
I pick up the pieces
that are left and invite
my guest to feel their
Sharpened edges,
But all challenge me
to move ahead, not to
hold onto the pain
From the sharpened pieces.

That night, as I lay asleep in our motel room, I was suddenly awakened by Lisa's hand shaking my shoulder. 'Are you alright? Are you all right, Candy?" she asked. As I sat up in bed, Lisa continued, "What were you screaming about?"

"Dreaming," I thought to myself," was I dreaming?" Then the dream re-entered my mind.

All that I had thought was left behind on the ending day had come back again to haunt me in the night. But I couldn't tell Lisa what had made me scream out in my sleep.

"Just a dream of the ocean," I answered, after my thoughts were pulled back together. "You know, I guess my first day in the ocean had a bigger impact than I thought," I continued.

"Well, go back to sleep, and see if you can't put the ocean out of your mind till tomorrow. Maybe we can start the day off better tomorrow. I wouldn't want you to be screaming every night we are here," she laughed.

"Sorry about that. But what are friends for, but to be awakened by their roommates in the middle of the night?" I added to the laughter.

I couldn't tell her about my childhood; it wasn't the right time, and I wasn't sure what I would tell her. It would start with my father's anger, and I wasn't sure if

I understood enough to even begin to explain that to her yet.

I was awakened the next morning with the thoughts of the night clouding my mind, but as I rolled over to get out of bed, I could see the sun beaming in through a crack in the curtain. "Bright sun rays of new beginning," I thought in my mind, as I arose from the bed to get a better look at what the sun was bringing to the day. I gently pulled back enough of the curtain to get a look at the morning's picture. The sun had brought out an early riser seeking the treasures that had been left behind from the ocean's spill the night before.

"What are you doing up already?" Lisa asked from her bed.

"I didn't think you would be up till noon after your dream last night." She added.

"I was awakened by the sun beaming its bright invitation to the day through the crack in the curtain," I said.

"It is only 6:30 in the morning," Lisa groaned. "Can't you give a friend a break? First, the screaming in the night, and now the sun. I say you go back to bed and give yourself at least till 10 before you start the day." Lisa yawned. "The sun will be higher, and we can take in some of its rays to start that sun-tan we came after."

But the sun on the ocean had my full attention now.

"I think I will just sit out on the patio for a while; you go ahead and catch up on your sleep," I announced without turning away from the view.

"OK, but don't let me sleep too long," she laughed, knowing somehow that wouldn't be the case. I opened the sliding glass door that led to the patio; there were two chairs and a table made of plastic table. A black iron rail was the only thing to protect me from the ocean, but somehow I knew this day would bring back better feelings.

The warm sun felt like it had already made its climb to high noon. Its warmth on my face drew at my soul, drawing me on to take a closer look at what it was shining its light on. Its beam shone on the ocean's waves of white cascades reflecting like a mirror, making it difficult to focus on all the water had to offer.

People walked with bags in hand; they were in hopes of finding treasures. Joggers took in the ocean's shores, enduring the hard surfaces to shape their bodies for the days to come. And there was I trying to draw the warmth that the sun had brought to void out the memories of the day before. But how could I forget the pain that I felt…? Too many things had happened in my childhood.

The chairs and table, boxed off with bars, reminded me of the time when I went to visit my father in the hospital. His room had only two chairs and a table. It also had bars on the door. Why was my father there? Why was my father locked up?

I heard the glass door open from behind me. Then a voice followed.

"I guess you thought I would let you have this all to yourself," Lisa interrupted.

"There is enough here for both of us," I assured her.

"Isn't it beautiful? The sun gave me a day with a new invitation to view the ocean once again."

"Does that mean you are going to try the water today?" Lisa asked. "We can buy some boards or rent them and get a feel of the waves today." She added.

"I think I had had a pretty good feel of that yesterday; don't you?"

"Come on, Candy, put that behind you and start again," Lisa pleaded. But little did Lisa what that's what I had tried to do for years.

I wanted to put the years behind me that I could not change. My father's death was the final say in that, because questions could not be answered as to why he lived such a angry life, and why we couldn't have a better understanding of each other's needs. I cried at my father's funeral, because at that time my feelings told me to hate him for the angry words he so violently screamed out, and for those angry blows he dealt each of his sex children. Somehow, maybe he wanted us to feel the impact life had dealt him. But then, too, I cried because

I wanted to know why I couldn't please him in all the years I had tried. Why couldn't we have the relationship that other fathers and daughters had? I knew what the "Ten Commandments" stated: "Honor Thy Mother and father…," but how could I live up to this unless I honored every blow he hurled at me?

I suddenly realized that old memories had led me away from the warmth of the sun, and I knew somehow that Lisa was right; I would have to keep trying to put it behind me. At that moment, I knew I had to come to grips with my thoughts and let this vacation give me the renewal it was meant to give.

"Come on Lisa yelled with excitement, "let's get breakfast over with before you change your mind."

We fixed bagels and coffee; that is, we shared a bagel. Lisa had some idea that we were here to refresh or reshape our bodies while we were on vacation. Our meals would be just enough to give us the energy to do our four-mile walk for the day, but Lisa never figured on the water giving us a stronger appetite than she had in mind. How could we lose? With this vacation, we were going to reshape our thirty-eight-year-old bodies and, in the process, lose our minds or reshape them too. We ate our breakfast out on the patio so as not to miss a moment of the sun's energy.

There was no time for cleaning up the dishes, because Lisa didn't believe in a clean room on vacation. I somehow agreed to that, but I knew the horrible end would be dishes stacked high until we had to wash them, or go out for meals. We both sat there for a few moments after we finished our coffee.

"Let's hit the waves," Lisa yelled.

We put our suits on in a hurry and found ourselves eager to be reintroduced to the ocean's power.

We rented boards and found ourselves in the water sooner than I thought we would be, but this time the waves weren't as powerful. This gave me a little more confidence. Just what I needed to enjoy this day.

Fear

The ocean with all its power
Had taken something away from me
Yesterday, but today it had given me
A sense of understanding.

That fear can be put to rest by trying again, and
freedom can come into the smallest forms.

L isa plunged right in. She was out in the waves before I knew she was gone. She suddenly returned with her board in hand and announced her first wave had been tackled.

"That wasn't bad. Come on, Candy, just catch the next wave from where you are standing, and let yourself enjoy it."

I grabbed my board and waited for the challenge with fear in the back of my mind. "I have to do this," I thought to myself. "List is right, I just need to catch the next wave."

"Here it comes; get ready," Lisa yelled.

I tried not to think about how the outcome would be. Then suddenly I found myself on top of the water with the shore coming closer and closer and the water getting shallower and shallower. When I finally realized what had happened, Lisa was at my side, jumping up and down and yelling. "You did it, You did it! I can't believe you finally put your fears behind you and did it!"

The word "fear" echoed in the air until it caught my attention; I knew it hadn't fully escaped me, but I just felt a feeling of freedom I had not experienced before.

The ocean, with all its power, had taken something away from me yesterday, but today it had given me a sense of understanding. That fear can be put to rest by trying again, and freedom can come to you in the smallest forms.

"You ready to try again? Lisa asked in an eager voice.

"Go ahead, I will be right behind you," I answered.

Lisa grabbed a hug and ran in to catch the next wave.

"Don't forget to watch behind you, Candy; you know

You have to be ready at the right moment," she reminded me.

I couldn't believe I had just told her I would do this again. Was I crazy? Or had the ocean finally given me some comfort of understanding?

"Look out!" I heard a voice from behind. Don't turn your back on the water, or you will be at the bottom again."

Lisa now reminded me of the power again, and suddenly the thoughts haunted my mind of the times I had turned my back on my father and felt the power he had, but I wouldn't let this take the feeling of freedom and wholeness away I had just experienced. No, I wouldn't let the past come back to spoil this moment of renewal between me and the ocean. Fully aware of the waves, I grabbed my board and found myself on top of the water, and the memories that haunted me vanished from my mind. Lisa was right beside me now, and her face was filled with excitement.

"Hold on," she cautioned, "This is the challenge of the day. If we conquer this one, we are home free and ready for the beach and the sun rays." Lisa knew little of my thoughts I had put behind me, but she was right: if I conquered this one, it would be the first step for me into a process of letting go.

The wave came closer and closer. Lisa turned her board toward the beach. I looked at her, and she motioned me on. I put my body full length of the board, as the waves came from behind me. It pushed me to the top of its back. I put my hands out to my sides. The water glided me along. My thoughts were, "How could something give me such a feeling of freedom to be so powerful?" This was the freedom I yearned for as a child. Free to turn your back on the world and it not come tumbling down on you. We made it to the shore all in one piece, and Lisa said, our reward was waiting for us there. The sun's invitation was still open, and it was welcome after all the excitement. We spent an hour sunning from side to side, and then we walked up and down the beach until I thought my legs would not carry me back to the room. I didn't want to give up this day so easily, because I knew tomorrow would be our last. I knew that my childhood memories that had been brought to the surface by the strong touch of the ocean's hands would have to be dealt with when I returned home, because there was too much I had been hiding about the hard knocks of my father's hands and harsh knocks of my father's voice in the past and the present. There would be too many echoes from my brother's and sister's pain to allow me to avoid my needs any longer.

The pain they so often spoke of, but the pain I thought only belonged to them and not me. The childhood pain that I had blocked out until now.

We made it back to our room, but I don't know how; I guess it was on the energy we created from the excitement we shared. I do know it wasn't in the fuel our breakfast had given us, because my stomach was telling me it was empty. As we entered the elevator, Lisa announced that she was hungry. Then my stomach replied with a groan before I had the chance to answer, Lisa began to laugh.

"What is so funny?" I asked, laughing too.

"I think you are trying very hard to starve us on this trip."

"Now what whatever gave you that idea?" she continued, laughing.

"Because." I said, laughing harder now with only a little energy left, "Sharing a bagel and a cup of coffee is not my idea of breakfast."

"Well, I am just trying to help you stay fit, but if you want, tomorrow you can have your bagel."

With both of us laughing harder now, as the door opened, we started to step out without looking, just like we were in our little world, but suddenly we realized that we were face to face with a gray-headed, bearded, old man, and that we weren't the only ones staying at this motel.

"Excuse me," Lisa and I said at the same time, and we took opposite paths around him to finish our exit.

"Close call!" we both announced. We were both giggling so hard that we couldn't get the key to go into the lock on the door of our room. Suddenly, with our shoulders against the door, we both fell into the room.

"What's for lunch?" I asked, still laughing at the exit of the elevator and the entry into our room.

"We have leftovers from last night," Lisa announced. "We can share them."

"Sure, but only if we eat at a place where they have low-calorie food."

"Somehow, I knew there was a catch to this agreement.

It's a deal," I said.

We ate lunch and decided we were both too tired to do dishes again. We would save them for tomorrow since it would be our last day there.

"I think I could take a nap," Lisa announced. "For some reason, I didn't sleep well last night, and the morning started earlier than I thought it would," Lisa smiled with her words.

"Sounds good," I said.

We both slept soundly into the darkness of the night.

"Boy," Lisa announced with a stretch, "We both must have been tired."

"Guess so," I answered, not quite awake yet.

"We need to get up and start getting ready if we are going out to eat," Lisa said.

"Yes," I agreed, before she could change her mind and suggest leftovers instead. The South Carolina shores were famous for their fish dishes, and I wasn't going to eat leftovers and go home tomorrow without trying some native dishes of blackened shark and crab legs dipped in rich butter sauce.

Gale Winds

The winds stir as we leave
the shores of the ocean.
Always the gale winds with the
upper hand to lead me away from
the ocean's strong wanting
Power.

The night had come sooner than we both had wanted it to because we knew tomorrow would be here before we knew it. Then we would have to say goodbye to the ocean shores. After supper, we went back to our rooms to change our clothes for a walk on the beach. I knew Lisa's motive wasn't just to take in the beauty of the ocean at night, but to torture me for overeating.

But when we reached the beach, things had begun to change. As I walked along the strand of ocean, I could see that the beach was larger than before. It was as if the water had been absorbed by something. Little did I know, it was low tide. We could walk farther out now, without the waves splashing on us. Even though the beach appeared to be unfamiliar, I knew I had walked there that day. The ocean had withdrawn from the activities on the beach. I could feel a quietness in the air. It was as if the ocean had nothing to say. As I continued my walk, I could see that things were beginning to change. A storm was blowing in, and I could see black clouds moving in. The rain started to beat against my face as it came roaring across the water. The ocean was awakened by the changes, and it seemed to be opening its mouth, letting the water fill the beach more and more. By this time, night was in full command, and the strand was covered with water. The ocean tossed its water about even strongly now, as the rain disappeared. I could see that the ocean was at high tide, and there was a full moon that had been hiding behind the clouds. The water sparkled under its glow. As I got closer and closer to the ocean's mouth, I could hear it talking again and the sounds were loud and strange to my ears. It was as though the ocean had been angered by something or someone. Then the haunting thoughts started filling my mind again. Could it be that I had brought my anger to the ocean's waters and now it was trying to spill it back at me?

Something caught my attention as I walked onward, and my thoughts were frozen in time. There before me were fish popping up like popcorn in a pan, close to the beach. I could see this really well by the floodlights shining out over the ocean, from the buildings along the strand.

In front of me, as I walked, two men tried to launch a small boat into the water. The waves kept tossing them back, as if they were trying to keep them out of the water for some reason. They finally won over the ocean and tackled the waves.

I could feel a strange heaviness in the air now. The tides became larger and larger, and the wind began to join in the anger. It sounded like they were talking to each other in loud, threatening voices.

I walked back to my room, unaware that Lisa had been walking with me all this time. I wanted to view the ocean at a distance, but things did not change. The tides were still high, and the beach seemed to be no more. What had I done? The ocean's anger was unfamiliar to me, and somehow, I thought I had brought my anger to its shores. It kept drawing my attention, but in all its anger, it didn't seem like anyone else was listening to it. I knew so well what could happen if I turned my back on the anger that was there. If Lisa was aware of my change in mood, she didn't question it.

We both watched the ocean until the strand seemed to disappear.

"Come on," Lisa coaxed, "we have to pack for our trip home tomorrow." I knew now she was not aware of the feelings I was experiencing. She had no idea that I thought I had brought this anger to these shores. But what could I do about this? My heart once again felt like it had experienced the sharp blows my father had given me in anger.

I left the ocean the next day; my vacation was over. But the ocean's anger had just started. It grew and grew until it developed into a hurricane. It took over beaches and homelands. The rage was felt all up and down the coastline. The history of the past has been restored in the town of Charleston, South Carolina, so visitors good share in their history. Now these same buildings were destroyed by the rage of the hurricane. Their past had been kept for people to visit and share, but now it only reminded me of the past I wanted to destroy. I watched as the angry words reappeared that I had once heard from the lips of children and women and men, flashing across my television screen at home. It was like a rerun of the past. My heart was not there with them, even though I could feel the sharp, piercing stab to my chest. I knew things could never be right again. The ocean's shores had given me a feeling of freedom, I needed, but what had been the cost of my feelings of freedom? Lives and homes had been destroyed, and now the anger was returning to my soul in desperate need to find the peace the ocean's waters gave me!

Now, there was a new understanding to be found in the anger that I thought I had transferred to these people. I must return to the South Carolina ocean to get the answers to the questions I now have. I had to understand how I could transfer my anger into other people's lives. Hurricane Hugo had torn through the South Caroline towns in mid-September of 1989, changing the lives of many forever, but how could I have transferred my anger to these waters? I stood in darkness, waiting for winter to take the last breath of life from the elms and the maples that stood in the grove across from my home. I could not deny that change had started all around me, but as always, I wished time could stand still, so I could catch up with what little life I had left in me. The skies took on a gray color, and I felt winter drawing closer and closer as the days grew shorter. I tried desperately to understand the change, but without knowing how to share my secrets, I drew my body closer and closer into a small cocoon. I searched through each word that was spoken at every church function. I was looking for a way out of the pain that had taken over my world.

Messenger

There was a message being written by an artist, the wind, but it could never get it perfect, so it kept erasing and starting over again.

Once in my Sunday school class, they spoke of anger, and I especially remember one of the women voicing her opinion on anger, "God does not get angry," she said. "He does not think anger should be a part of anyone's life. There should be no anger in this world." I listened with eagerness thinking she might have found the answer to all of my problems "We should take that energy and put it into something more constructive." The words she had spoken seemed to be going in the right direction, but when the word, "constructive" entered the room, I knew she was on the right trail. The ocean had been so destructive, destroying homes and lives, but how could this apply to my father's anger? I now started searching harder and harder for the answers I needed to put my life back on track.

Spring crept closer and closer, and I found more evidence in other people's words, and in the words of the Bible. My shell seemed to crack open to meet the new beginning of spring. Birds sang songs I hadn't heard in an awfully long time. The elms turned green again, and the maples wore more and more leaves each day. My world was opening up again. The news spoke of new beginnings for South Carolina' there would be new construction. Hearing that, I longed to go back to the shores of the Atlantic ocean.

In midsummer, the telephone rang.

"Hello," I answered.

"Hi, Candy," said a familiar voice.

"Are you ready to go on vacation again? I am ready to start planning a trip."

"Yes," I answered without any hesitation. I couldn't wait to touch the cool sand on the shores of the South Carolina beaches. I wanted more than ever to reconnect my feelings with the new construction that was taking place there.

"How about we go some place different this year?" I heard Lisa say. "Maybe we could try South Padre Island. It is beautiful there. With the hurricane last year at Myrtle Beach, I think we ought to give them time to rebuild before we go back."

My heart now felt the sharp pain again that hadn't been felt since the hurricane hit. Then I couldn't believe the words that were coming out of my mouth. "That sounds good," I answered. "New, I guess, is good, Lisa."

"You don't sound like that is what you want to do."

"No, I mean, yes, it sounds like a change could be good."

"We can go back to South Carolina next year if our husbands will still let us go, she laughed. I'll get some information on the trip and get back with you. Got to go now. I will talk with you soon."

I hung up the phone trying to put the whole picture before me. Next year probably would be better for our trip back to South Carolina. It would give the residents more time to build, and maybe things will look the same again. Just maybe the TV and radios were wrong about the damage the people on the beaches had encountered. The people on TV like to exaggerate sometimes.

I settled into the new idea and okayed it with my husband and boys. Of course, they had to start their usual teasing about my leaving them all by themselves, but I didn't let them put a guilt trip on me, like I so often had before.

Time seemed to fly by and Lisa had put the airplane tickets in the mail. I was starting to get eager about the trip. This could be good for me, I thought, a different look at the world and how other people lives.

Next thing I knew, I found myself soaking up sun rays on Padre Island thinking about the days before the trip.

I had stayed to myself most of the summer keeping people at a distance, but trying to draw out of their lives what my life needed. But that wasn't easy, because I still wasn't sure what that could be. Lisa and I arrived at our hotel in time to have some time in the sun. The Island was so different than that of the South Carolina. There were no homes next to the ocean, only motels and businesses. It was as if the owners knew about the destructive anger that the ocean could spew out. The sun in its burning orange dress felt hotter than that of South Carolina shores. My head started to throb with pain of exhaustion from the flight there and the heat added to my announcement.

"List, I think I will go back to the room for a nap. My head is pounding and I think I am just tired for all the excitement of the trip."

"I am glad you spoke up, I am tired too; a nap sounds good," Lisa said. "We can rest for a couple of hours and then get something to eat, and maybe take in some sights," Lisa finished.

The nap and the sights sounded good, but Lisa hadn't changed our diets from last trip, so I knew what she meant about eating. Leftovers or diet food, eek!

Even though I was very tired and my heard felt like it was splitting open, I couldn't put the sights we had seen on the way there out of my mind. Most of the homes were low-income housing and the doors and windows all had bars on them. What were these people trying to keep out? Had they found the solution to the problem? Bars could most certainly keep out the anger that could be outside their homes, but what if it was lurking inside waiting to come out?

With that uneasy thought, I feel asleep, but my dreams kidnapped me back to my childhood once again. Darkness was all around me, and I could hear my father's voice get louder and louder. I had escaped to my cocoon again—a small place I had found by crawling through a hole in our foundation that led to a small space up inside of our staircase. Even though the sounds were still there, I knew I was safe because no one else could fit into my sanctuary. I was only about eight or nine at the time. My father's anger would grow and grow and then my mother's voice would scream out the pain he had dealt her. But after a while all would get silent again. I never knew if it was safe to come out, but even at that age I would pray the whole time that the anger was flowing, for God to put an end to the loud voices. The dimness would sometimes become even darker and I would know that night had crept in. Now I would have two fears to face—more darkness and my father's voice again demanding to know where I had been. These stairs that I found refuge in were the same exact stairs I would sit on, praying and pleading for God to send my mother and father home, so they could put order back into my life after leaving me with my brother and sisters all day. Suddenly I woke up from my nap to find Lisa still fast asleep. I was chilled by the dream and by the air conditioned room, so I quietly crept outside to our patio to draw heat and light from the sun. It was beautiful there! The sun gave me a sense of security and that was what I needed to void out my dream of the darkness.

"What's up>" I heard a voice from behind me.

"I can't believe I slept that long," Lisa said.

"I know—I just got up myself. We must have both been more tired than we thought we were," I added.

"I can't wait to see the rest of this island. If it's anything like this ocean, we have made a good choice of our vacation spot this year."

Suddenly Lisa's words were interrupted by the horn from an in-coming boat. "I guess they are back with the day's catch," Lisa suggested.

"Speaking of the day's catch, Lisa, how about we get ready and go get something to eat and take in those sights you wanted to see?"

"Are you trying to tell me something, Candy, or is it my imagination running wild? Could it be that you don't' want to eat our food we shopped for?"

"I guess you could come to that conclusion," I answered, now starting to laugh. Lisa an I could always find a way to make each other laugh, even in the darker moments.

"Okay," Lisa answered, "but I get the shower first."

"Fine with me." I needed the time alone to put my dream in order. What had made me dream about my father again? Had it been the darkness I had seen and felt around this island? Now I knew more than ever that I had to start the process of taking down the bars that held my angry memories inside of me. I had to start to trust the idea that I was not to blame for his anger and that by keeping people out of that side of my life, I could only keep bringing back the pain.

"Your turn," I heard Lisa yell from the room through the crack she had left in the patio door.

"Hurry up, before I change my mind about eating out," she laughed.

I was glad to get the interruption, but now I had put the process in motion. "No way," I answered you're not going to back out on our deal. First a good meal then the sights."

"What do you think will be our choice for supper?" I asked Lisa. With that I entered the bathroom, so she could think in silence. I turned the shower water on just as I heard her mumble some kind of answer. "It will keep" I thought, "I had better hurry up before she changes her mind." I stepped into the shower and closed the streaked glass door behind me. Darkness fell over me again as the hot steam suddenly clouded the light.

My father's vision and his words came stumbling in at me again. "Why can't you do anything right?" he screamed at me. "I asked you to do a simple thing and this is the results. That shower door looks worse than it did before!" He shook his fist at me in rage. "You go back in there and clean it again and don't come out until it is spotless. You hear me?" He screamed. I kept hearing the word "spotless" repeatedly until the spell was broken by Lisa's voice.

"Hurry up in there," she yelled, "I am hungry".

I wiped my face, turned off the shower and stepped out into the lighted room, but the lingering thoughts sent a chill to my bones. "Hungry, yes, I was hungry too," I said to myself as I tried to wipe the thoughts from my mind.

We both finished getting dressed and went downstairs, to be greeted at the front door by the bell-hop dressed in a white and name blue trimmed suit. "Let's ask him if he knows where we can eat," Lisa suggested.

"If you want fish, the Sea Shore's Restaurant is nice and the price is right, but if you want Mexican food, the Hold In The Wall Bar is the place to go. It doesn't look like much from the outside but the food is the best on the Islands." He stated. We were not far from the Mexican border and the bell-hop was Mexican. In fact, that is how you could tell the tourists from the people who lived there.

"Mexican food sounds good to me, Lisa, how about you?" I asked.

"Why did I know that is what you would want?" Lisa laughed.

"Okay, Mexican it is."

I drove, while Lisa searched for the bar. It wasn't far from the motel. "Are you sure we want to go in there?" I asked.

"The bell-hop was right." Lisa answered, "It isn't much for looks."

"Oh, come on let's try it; no one knows us here, so we can leave if we don't like the inside of it."

We both slowly opened the door to the bar to find just what the name implied—a hole in the wall. It was decorated with fish nets and sampros and country western music played in the background. "What do you think?" Lisa asked softly just before the waitress greeted us.

School Bus

Left alone to rust away
the yellow body that once
held thousands of minds filled
with knowledge.

Abandon to rust away
The knowledge it carried…
The memories of voices
that echoed the cry of
The young.

The wisdom of thought
Now hollow and cold…
Now stuck in the same…
Now unnoticed by many…

The bus reflects the warmth
from the sun as the sand
cradled it in its hands.

Sometimes looks aren't the best advertisement, either. She wore a mini-skirt with a sheer silk blouse, and her makeup could have stopped a horse in its tracks. Lisa and I had to hold our laughs for later because the place was so small, our reactions would have been noticed. The menus were full of calories, just as we both had suspected they would be, but we both ordered a sample plate so as not to miss any of it. The bellhop was right. The food was excellent, and Lisa and I agreed we had eaten too much.

"Let's take our leftovers back to our room," Lisa suggested. We can finish them off for lunch tomorrow."

"You mean I get to eat good food again tomorrow?" I laughed.

"Yes, I guess," and Lisa joined in with the laughter. "But, we have to walk some of this food off before we go back to our rooms," she added.

We left the bar and decided to ride around for a while.

"This island is so small," I announced, after a few miles down the road. "It isn't anything like South Carolina, is it Lisa?"

"No," she answered. "Let's take that road down the coast," she said. The road followed the ocean, but after a few miles, we could see it led to only a dead end. "Stop!"

Lisa yelled. "Look what is over there behind that sand dune."

I stopped the car and pulled up onto the sandy shoulder. There as an old yellow school bus that had bee left there to rust. "Com on," Lisa yelled as she got out of the car, "let's get a closer look."

"Okay, but wait for me. You never know what could be lurking inside that bus."

As we got closer we could see it had been left vacant for the summer, but we could also tell that someone had used it not too long ago. There was cardboard on the windows and ashes from a fire were in the center of the bus's shell.

"I guess somebody could have taken shelter here," I found myself saying out loud.

"Yes," Lisa added, "this is probably a bus that someone used for transportation here to the islands, but after running out of money left it for something else that came along."

This bus reminded me of the late sixties, when the flower child era was in full swing, but it only started memories flowing to the surface again about my childhood. During the sixties my father was hurt at his job, and soon after that was forced to quit working. He became disabled, so he was around the house all the time and his presence was well felt by his angry voice greeting my every moment.

"Candy," Lisa interrupted, "let's go. This bus is spooky, don't you think?"

How well I thought that, but the bus was not my focus anymore, as I stood silently in the sand letting my mind fill with haunted memories again.

"We can drive further down the coast," Lisa broke in again as she turned to start back to the car.

"What were you in such deep thought about?" Lisa asked as we closed our car doors.

"Don't you think it is funny how some things can remind you of other things that are totally the opposite, Lisa?" I found myself blurting our loud. I couldn't believe I had even said that; now I would have to explain myself.

"Yes," Lisa answered, "it happens sometimes when you think you have put something out of your mind, only to have it come creeping back invading your world of the present place and time." I could hardly put the car key in the ignition. Had we made a break-through in what we both had to say or was it just an answer appropriate for the time?

Then my words cam without warning; they must have been on my lips before I even knew it. "Yes, there have been a lot of things invading my mind since my father's death," I heard my voice say.

"Death has a way of haunting you," Lisa answered. Lisa's first husband and died and now I was reminded of this. She had spoken the first words. Now I knew it would be an invitation to talk more if I needed to.

I finally got the car started and we drove further down the coast until both our eyes caught the same sight; there next to the ocean shore was an area that looked as if it were a graveyard for sea shells. "Stop," I heard Lisa say, "let's get a closer look." We both couldn't believe the sight. There were thousands—no maybe millions—of sea shells lying in the sane. My first thoughts were, "Where were all the treasure seekers we had seen on the shores at South Carolina? People couldn't wait to find their perfect shell there." Gut there was no one seeking these shells. Could it be that the ocean had discarded these shells like my father had discarded me. As Lisa and I got closer we could see that the shells had been there for a long time, because they were buried deep in the sand and stacked high.

"Maybe my father's love for me had been there. Deep down inside."

"Why wouldn't people want these shells?" I asked Lisa.

"Would you want something that is flawed?" Lisa was quick to answer.

"But if they took time to look closer, maybe they could find some good in them," I said. I suddenly realized something; that is what I had been doing all these years. I had been trying to find some good in my father's anger or something good in the way he treated me.

"But, sometimes there are flaws too de3ep," Lisa broke in. "And sometimes you can't change the way they are flawed even if you did take time to hunt for them. Let's see how many we can find that are in one piece," Lisa suggested. We both started our own search by going in different directions.

"Don't' get too far away," I warned Lisa; "You never know what could be lurking behind these sand dunes."

I found an old frame of a wooden hair brush to dig with. I just knew we could find some shells with life still in them to save from the ocean shore grave.

Suddenly the wind began to pick up and the air started to get coo. I looked up to see Lisa in the distance, and then as I looked back down I spied something different in the sand. There was a message being written by an artist, the wind, but it could never get it perfect, so it kept erasing and starting over again. What was going on in this graveyard?

Then a soft voice spoke, "What are you looking for girlie? There are no treasures here, only broken shells."

I lifted my head from my search to find a short, old lady wrinkled with age, wearing layers of tattered clothes. Her hair was dirty and I could tell it had been unattended for a long time. "There are no treasures here girlie," she repeated, as I looked to see where Lisa was.

"Where did you come from?" I found myself asking.

"From over there," she pointed without looking in that direction. "There are not reassures to find here," she spoke again. "I know, because I have searched and searched these shores," she added.

Just then I noticed she clutched a dirty shampoo bottle in her hand. "What is that?" I asked.

"Just a bottle," she answered as she clutched the bottle tighter to her body. "I found it in the trash."

By now Lisa had reached me and she interrupted with a "Hi.".

The old lady turned to face Lisa as I motioned my shoulder to let Lisa know I wasn't sure what her presence meant.

"Just telling the girlie that there are no treasures here," she repeated as she reached for Lisa's necklace.

"We aren't looking for treasures," Lisa explained. "We are just trying to get a few shells to take back home"

"You girlies better be careful," she warned, ignoring Lisa's explanation.

Then as Lisa turned to walk closer to me, we both took our eyes off the old lady in question, and when we turned back, she was gone.

"Where did she come from," Lisa asked.

"I don't know, but better yet where did she go?"

"Not just yet," Lisa said. "I want to look in that direction for a while." She moved away from me and I started my search again.

But, it was only two or three steps from where the artist had been writing, that I dug up a shell. It had the pattern of clouds on its back and the marks of sea gulls with their wings spread wide for flight. It was tan and beige and the shape was not without flaws. I thought I had found my treasure for the day. "Lisa," I yelled, "come and look at the shell I have found."

Lisa was closer than I had noticed so the wait was not long.

"That is a beauty," she said as she examined it. "I can't get that old lady off my mind," she added. "Maybe we better go. It is getting late and the lady's warning bothers me." We both picked up what we had gathered and headed for the car. Tomorrow would be our last day on the island and we wanted to make the most of what was left of the night by walking on the beach. As we left the sight of the sea shell behind us, we began to discuss the old lady that had come from out of no where. "That old lady sure was weather-worn," I reminded Lisa.

"She looked older than some of those shells. Where do you supposed she came from, Lisa?"

"I don't know, but she just appeared like magic and left in the same manner," Lisa offered.

"I think she looked like she belonged there. Maybe she was the caretaker for the grave-yard of shells," I added. "The grave-yard keeper," I thought to myself.

"But, why was she so sure there were no treasures there?" Lisa asked. "She was sure dead-set there weren't any."

"Maybe because she has been there longer than we can imagine," I told Lisa. "She was old-looking; maybe she has been looking for the perfect shell or treasure all these years and now she has come to the conclusion in her old age that there aren't any."

"You could be right, Candy, because who is to know what kind of treasures she has been looking for?"

Lisa was right. Who was to know what the old lady was looking for. No one knew how hard I had been trying to find some good in my father's abuse. This old lady could have gotten caught up in her search for something and grew old trying to fine it. Could this old lady be me if I didn't come to terms with the fact that there wasn't anything good about my father's beatings. But I felt so guilty, because I always thought when my father hit me I deserved it, or I caused his anger. My father's voice would make me shake every time he would say my name. This old lady sure made me think about the past I wanted to bury and forget.

We made it back to our motel-room and put tomorrow's lunch in the cooler we had bought.

"Ready for a walk on the beach?" Lisa asked.

"Sure," I answered. "Let's get going if we want to catch the guard, before he leaves with someone else."

Padre island was not like the shores of South Carolina. You had to be careful about what time of day you walked on the beach, so most people would get the security guards to watch them take their nightly swim or their last walk for the day. There were no treasures seekers at night trying to get the first find before morning, either. The night was beautiful as those we had found on the Atlantic shores, but the air was a little thicker and maybe a little stale.

Tonight the clouds out over the ocean seemed to be in a world all of their own—. A beautiful world of structure and form not seen back home. The moon only peeked its head out as the clouds would let it, and we couldn't fully decide if it was the moon at all. The rain came like sadness in our hearts as every form seemed to disappear behind the clouds doors. We walked back to our rooms with the rain on our faces, trying to hold back the tears that we knew had came early—for tomorrow we would say our good-byes to the ocean and the moments we spent there would have to last us at least a whole year.

The next year came and I looked forward to the reunion with Lisa and the time we would spend planning our vacation back to South Carolina.

Then, it happened. One day I received a letter from Lisa explaining how sorry she was, but she would have to change jobs and the vacation would have to wait another year. Could this really be happening again? I had made it through the dreary winter months only to e told our vacation would have to be put on hold.

I found a void in the next months to come. I felt more like a snail moving slower and slower in no certain direction. I listened every day for some news of South Carolina on the TV, but little information came in, if any at all. How could people forget about something so destructive? People's lives had been changed and rearranged and now no one cared. It had been two years cine I had walked the beaches of the Atlantic Ocean, but my memory would not erase the fear that I saw in the desk clerk's eyes when Lisa and I had checked out of the motel. It reminded me of my own fear when I knew the time was getting closer for my father's arrival home from work. How could she speak of the hurricanes in the past like they had been just storms the people on the strand had weathered, but somehow even though I could not imagine the impact, I could see the strain on her face. Hugo's impact had been just like the force I had so often felt from my father's hands. It had knocked everything off-balance.

My memories now invaded me again, and I suddenly felt like I was on an island destined to sink. How could my mind hold all these thoughts that kept floating to the surface? My father had beat me whenever things didn't go just right for him. If he didn't abuse me with his hands, he was verbally abusing me. He always made fun of my figure or the way I talked.

"You talk like Donald Duck; you walk so pigeon toed it's a wonder you don't fall over your own feet"

As time passed on slowly, I grew wisdom from my sisters and brothers hurts of their childhood. They had all shared their pain of our father's anger. Each one of them had been abused. My brothers had been made to quit school at an early age and take on more work than they should. My father played them against each other by showing favorites. My next to the oldest brother was kind of like me. He could never please my father no matter what he did. My oldest sister was my father's angel. She could do nothing wrong. But even she had some anger for my father. My father had left his mark on all of us. But I knew we would each have to find our own way of bringing our memories to our own level of understanding. How could I feel so much blame for my father's violence. Was it because, I wanted to protect my family from him. Is that why I wanted to go back to South Carolina? Was I feeling the pain for these people or was I feeling my father's pain that had been often put out of my mind, like the hurricane had gone out to sea and was forgotten about, until something stirred it up again?

Time seemed to stand still for the longest time, but not without its reward. Lisa had now contacted me and our trip was going to be a go this year. My whole body signed with relief. A chance to put things back in the right perspective again. I knew if I could get back to the ocean's waters I could draw a final end to this pain that still ached in my heart. Maybe even an end to the memories that were etched in my mind. I really couldn't tell at this point if it was the memories of the people back in South Carolina.

Finally the day had come for me to pick up Lisa for the ride to the airport. I stayed only long enough to put her suitcase in the trunk and we were off.

"I can't wait to see the ocean," I found myself telling Lisa with eagerness in my words.

"Me too, Lisa replied, "It's been a long time since we walked on the shores of the Atlantic Ocean."

"I know, I don't know how I ever made it through two winters," I added; winter is such a dark time and you can get depressed so easy with things lying dead all around you. It is even harder when you feel like life has been knocked out of you so many times you can't find a way to get your spirits back."

"You sound like you know what you are talking about, Candy. It sounds like to me you have traveled down some pretty rough roads in life."

Our trip hadn't even gotten off the ground yet, and Lisa was drawing me out of my shell that I had chosen to hid in like a hermit crab.

"I could tell you about a few painful moments in my life, Lisa, but let's not get the tears of joy flowing just I warned.

We made the airplane, and Lisa suggested we have a drink to celebrate our trip.

I declined. "No way am I going to get off this plan with my feet half under me." I said I wanted to save the celebration for our first look at the ocean and all the sights. I knew things would be different, but somehow just to touch the water that had once been my greatest fear would reassure me that there was still some life in me.

We both struggled to get the suitcase to the elevator. "Why do we always do this?" I asked Lisa. "We always seem to over-pack."

"Who over-packed?" Lisa questioned. "Not me—I am doing fine with my luggage. You are the one who over- packs. We could probably both live out of your suitcase," she laughed.

"Hurry up, so we can get to the beach," I insisted. "We still have some sun and I can't wait any longer."

By that time Lisa and I had arrived at our room. She put the key in the door and we both took one deep breath and fell inside our room.

"How about that entry?" Lisa laughed "you can't hurry any faster than that!" By the time Lisa had the words out of her mouth, I was half way to the sliding glass doors to the patio; we always got an ocean-front view, so we could enjoy every minute of the ocean.

"It's even more beautiful than I remembered it," Lisa and I said, as we both took in as much as we could see from side to side.

"It is so quiet;" Lisa spoke. "I don't remember the ocean every being so quiet, she continued.

Lisa was right, we had left the ocean while it was almost at its full peak of anger and now it was as calm as if nothing had happened.

"Look," Lisa pointed to the beach houses down the coast, "it doesn't look like anything happened to those homes!" she exclaimed.

But how could that be possible? I thought. "There was no way that kind of anger could have exploded and not touched those homes," I replied.

"You really sound like you know what you are talking about," Lisa said.

"I do." Then suddenly I knew I would probably have to back that statement up, but for now I would change the subject. "Come on, Lisa. Last one dressed for the beach has to carry the groceries back from the store." I ran in ahead of her, but then as I looked back, I could still see Lisa standing looking out over the waters of the Atlantic Ocean.

"Don't think we will shop for our food this time," she announced. She had my full attention now.

What, Lisa, no health food for our over-weight bodies?

"No, let's just get soda and fruit and let each day turn out the way it does. Let's not set any rules on this trip."

"What had gotten into Lisa? She had finally gotten soft on me. Then I remembered the soft sand on the beach, and I answered Lisa with a sigh. "Sure, Lisa, that sounds good."

As I approached the ocean's mouth, I could hear that it had taken on a new voice. It greeted us with its soft white waves and a warm smile came quickly from its neighbor, the sun. I could see that the anger had left now, and the beach gave no evidence that it had ever been there. I knew somehow that it couldn't have totally vanished form this ocean shore. Things aren't just erased that easily.

"Come on," Lisa yelled, "let's go for a walk and see how much things have changed." We walked our usual direction, but the farther down the coast we went, things began to change a little. There was no green grass in between some of the motels and the beach. All we could see was sand piled up high.

"What has happened?" I said to Lisa. "IT looks like something has killed all the grass around here." Death seemed to be invading our every step.

"You think they could have planted more grass here," Lisa said, "and hauled off some of the left-over sand."

"It's as though some people care and some don't," I continued. Then my words stuck in my mind. I now had realized some people had given up after the hurricane hit— Not only on the removal of the sane but as I looked farther I could see some houses had not been repaired. My thoughts started surfacing again to the days of Padre Island. The shells had been cast away by the ocean and now these homes had been touched by the ocean's anger and people had left them to decay like the shells. Then my thoughts took me back further, this is how my father had left me. My soul had started to decay with bad memories, when I felt like I couldn't overcome the power of them. Lisa and I finished our walk on the beach, and somehow I knew this trip could only have new beginnings in store for me. I realized I didn't want to leave my memories locked up inside of me anymore.

I was right. The next day I awoke in darkness still. I knew what I wanted—I had to see my first sunrise out over the ocean. I quietly slid the glass door open and sneaked outside to our patio, trying not to wake Lisa. There it was, but no in full form yet. It reminded me of a double sunrise shell when it is fully closed. It took my breath away. I knew it could only be the creation of One—A Gift from God. It was a perfect gift. "The camera," I thought, "a gift this special has to be shared." I knew Lisa would never let me off the hook if I woke her up. I quietly got my camera. When I got back, the shell had started to open its mouth pulling the sun to its heights of full form. I watch in awe. This was already starting off to be a good day and I was starting to put the memories of the abandoned houses out of my mind. I sat on the patio in silence listening to the sea gulls fight over yesterday's leftovers. It reminded me of the days Lisa and I shared our leftovers. What had made Lisa give up our old menus?

Then I heard a voice from the room. "Candy, what are you doing out there?"

"I have just witnessed the most beautiful sunrise I have ever seen, Lisa.

"Why didn't you wake me up?" she yawned.

"Wake you up? Are you crazy? I wouldn't dare, not after the last trip we had here!"

"What are you talking about?" she asked.

"You don't remember the screams in the night and the early wake=up call I gave you?"

"Well, maybe I do remember something about that."

"Come on out and I will put the coffee on. You wait on me, that's a first. Oh quit your grouching, before I change my mind," I laughed.

"You are right," I heard Lisa say from the patio. "This is a beautiful sun today. We ought to be able to get the suntan we want today."

"Lisa," I said as I handed her the coffee, "How hard to you think the beach was really hit?"

"Well, what did the newspapers say," Lisa asked.

"I don't believe everything the news tells you. They can blow things up."

"This has really become a personal problem with you, hasn't it, Candy?"

"Well, I guess you can say that. I mean these people and I have something in common."

"Well, I certainly hope so," Lisa laughed, "We aren't any different than they."

"But Lisa, you don't understand. When I left here, I left something behind."

Lisa was now sitting straight up in her seat.

"Well, they would have sent it to you Candy, all you had to do is call the motel and tell them what it was."

"But I didn't want it back—I mean I didn't meant to leave it."

Then the words just seemed to flow out as fast as the angry ocean had over the beaches.

"You see, Lisa, sometimes to know someone isn't really to know that person in his or her true self."

"You have my full attention, Candy, go on."

"When I left here, I left my anger with all these people. The ocean kept trying to spill it back at me; I finally won and I left it to spill out on these people. Don't you understand, Candy? I left my father's anger here."

Now I did have her full attention. My eyes could not hold back some of the moisture that had begun to surface.

"But you can't leave someone's anger for other people to be hurt by," she said.

"Yes, you can, Lisa;" my voice seemed to shake now." You see, Lisa, my father used to take his anger out on me and anyone else in his path. From an early age I can remember him beating me and yelling, always yelling, and I don't know what kind of abuse he dealt my sisters or brothers, because I would always hide if I could."

Lisa now began to cry. "All these years, Candy. We have been friends all these years and you have never let on."

"I couldn't. I was too afraid to say anything to anyone. Then when my father died, the memories seemed to overpower me. I didn't know what to do. I tried to let go of them, but there were too many of them to deal with. It just seemed like I let all of life die around me. I couldn't put the memories out of my mind. Don't you see that is why I had to come back here? I thought I had brought the anger here." You see Lisa, the first year we visited the ocean my childhood memories resurfaced. My father's anger came rushing in on me when the tides took me under. The waves kept slapping at my body with so much power. I saw my father again knocking me to the ground. My life seemed to pass before me. But the past was the first thing to surface.

"I hate your father," Lisa said.

"No, I yelled," There has been too much anger and hate. I have to let go of these memories and set things right."

"But you have nothing to set right, Candy. These people knew what they were doing when they built here. They knew the chances they were taking. You had no choice; you were born into your father's anger and became caught up in it and even abused by it. You have to let go of it."

"That is why I needed to come back here. To start out with some kind of new beginning. I needed to see how these people coped with the anger the ocean tossed at them."

"But it's not the same, Candy. These people can rebuild if they want;' it is only material things that they lost. You have lost half your lifetime trying to figure something out that wasn't even your fault. You are right; you have to let go, and I know just how to get you started. Get your suit. The waves are calling us!"

I couldn't believe the hours that had slipped away while we were talking, but I had finally let the hermit out of the shell for good. Today would mark the first day of my free life. Time to hit the waves and let the ocean be the cure.

I thought I might get some writing in too, so I took my pad of paper with me. After Lisa and I conquered each wave we had tried for, I sat on the beach taking in each new breath of air. It felt good to have shared my secrets of my childhood with Lisa.

Suddenly, for the first time, I was aware of the different people on the beach. There was a man without any legs crawling to the ocean's waters and there was a lady that was dragging her overweight body to the ocean. "Why did these people come to the ocean?" I found myself asking.

"What was so beautiful about it? Then I knew the answer. It was another gift from God. God had the power to draw you in and the ocean was that power. God had drawn me back to the beginning of my fears and let be cry out in need like the people from the hurricane.

I knew now things would never be the same for the hurricane victims, but they had cried out in need and they had been heard around the world. Things are never the same after you have been touched by anger that has been hurled at you, but you can't stand still like the sea shells in the grave yard or you will start to decay. So the old has to become the new.

"What are you writing?" Lisa asked.

"Oh, just some notes on somethings."

"I have an idea: why don't we go out and celebrate tonight?"

"Sounds good to me" I replied.

Well, let's go so we can get ready for our celebration I am hungry."

Lisa and I went out to eat and then we went dancing. We met several nice gentlemen. Right before we left, they had a rose delivered to our table. I knew right away what I would have to do with the rose. Then a group of other people we met offered us a ride to our motel. We accepted. When we got to our building they asked if we would join them for a midnight walk on the beach.

The Rose

I give to you a red, red Rose
a petal at a time. You give to
me the beauty I see of
your gentle tides.

But your waters can not hold
the beauty that is so bold.

So, in a circle, I find each
Petal cast behind.

The thought of maybe a full moon had my attention. It couldn't have been more perfect for my last night there. The moon was showing off, and it had the sunrise beat hands down, but then it happened, the conversation led to Homeward Bound, and we shared with our company our family back home. The man who had drawn my attention had words of sadness in his voice, and of all the gifts that had been shared throughout this day, this one was most unusual. We were strangers to each other, but here we found ourselves like the moon shell that housed the snails. Moving slowly in one direction, sharing the sad stories about our lives.

You have to let go of things before they pull you under," he said. The man told me that he thought he had lost the only thing he ever loved by not knowing how to love, but out of his sorrow and hurt, he was taught to hold onto what he had and always value the gifts of life, even if it is dealt him sorrow and pain. "Sometimes I think God is testing us for a better part in life," he concluded.

Why did this gentleman come into my life at this time? I couldn't shake the feeling there was more to this than a soft conversation, but how did he know what to say? It was as though my life lay like the open ocean before us. Then the old lady came haunting back at me from Padre Island. I had to stop searching for the answer to my father's anger and the reason for the absence of his love. I had to move on with my life before I became old and life-worn like the grave-keeper. The thought of the old lady as a grave-keeper stuck in my mind. What if this lady were a sign of death? The death that could overcome me if I didn't move on with my life...This man had touched my soul—a part of me that had not been touched in a long time. My soul now felt like I could live again. It was time to put my fears completely behind me.

The next day would be my goodbye to the ocean, not knowing when I would return. I had one more thing to complete before I said goodbye. I took the red, red rose that had been given to me and walked it into the ocean deep, and let it go. I walked down the beach to get a last look. As I returned, the rose petals were lying in a circle with the stem lying bare in the center. I had given each petal of the rose to the ocean, casting all the years away that had been spent in pain and darkness, but the beauty of the ocean could not hold the years that stood so bold, so there was a message from its open mouth. That life must go on, and I must start new growth on the bare stem left now so gently. I knew that the first time I had met with the ocean, there was no understanding, and I walked the shores with disillusion, but now the pure white cascades sent out waves of gentleness. I knew

God's hands had touched my soul. My journey had led me around life's full circle.

I walked back down the beach, marking new footprints in the sand, and I knew this had marked the end of a new beginning. The ocean's anger had drawn me back, and I would take home the memories to share of new beginnings.

The Shell

The shell is empty now,
All has been exposed,
Solitude lies dormant inside
waiting for someone else
to take refuge there.

It has been a good place
sheltering me from the hurt
and pain, but as all comes
to an end. So does time.

Time to move on to a new
Place of unknown substance,
but as I slowly pack my heart
With the memories, I know,
I have to learn a lot from this place.

Patience, Kindness, Love.
Oh, yes even Forgiveness.

With my snail's pace, I know,
I will pick up other baggage
along the way, but one thing
I do know, as I look ahead
Hope has already started
moving into this direction

I have chosen…

9/13/93

Brenda J. Miller

About the Author

She has won several contests with her poetry and short stories. Ocean's Anger is her first finished manuscript. She belonged to the Missouri Writers' Guild for several years, and she was the President for the Jefferson County Writers' Guild and a member for several years also. She loves to write about her feelings and the true nature of the world around her. When her thoughts surface, it is hard to hold back what seems to be a natural gift to her, writing. Sometimes it is hard for her to see the writer in herself, because the words seem to be a gift from God. Her encouragement to write started with one English instructor at Jefferson College recognizing she had a gift and sense, then the encouragement of God, friends, and family has been her courage to move on to finish her education and to write.

She has finished her Bachelor of Science in Elementary Education, and she will soon finish her Master's Degree in Special Education. She uses her gift as a writer in her classroom to teach children about themselves and the world around them.

She has two sons and two grandchildren, and all are a breath of life to her writing.

www.ingramcontent.com/pod-product-compliance
Lightning Source LLC
Chambersburg PA
CBHW031231120626
46545CB00003B/1086